Fail Like a Pro.

17 Brutal Lessons They Don't Teach You About Cloud, Code, and Startup Life

Copyright

First Edition, 2025
ISBN: 9798281438681
Published by Souren Stepanyan
Printed by Amazon

For permissions or licensing inquiries, visit:
www.sourenstepanyan.com

Dedication

To every builder who failed silently,
fixed everything,
and kept going anyway.

This one's for you.
You're not invisible.

How to Use This Book

This is not a tutorial.
Not a checklist.
Not a polite DevOps guide wrapped in buzzwords and clickbait.

This is a field manual.

It's for when your system's on fire.
When your architecture's a mess.
When you're one crash away from quitting — or one launch away from something real.

Each chapter is a war story.
Each one holds something you can steal, adapt, or laugh about — ideally all three.

Read it in order.
Or don't.
You're already smarter than half the internet for reading anything this deep.

Just remember:
This book wasn't made to impress you.
It was made to outlast your next disaster.

About This Book

You won't find diagrams here.
You won't find corporate fluff.
And you sure as hell won't find another "10 steps to scaling your dream."

You'll find:

- Real failure.
- Real recovery.
- Real systems that survived just long enough to become legends — or warnings.

I wrote this for the ones who build with their hands, think with their guts, and live in terminal windows.

This isn't a blueprint.
This is a bloodstained map.

You've been warned.

Table of Contents

INTRODUCTION

Fail Like a Pro
(Or How I Learned to Stop Worrying and Love the Outage)

There's a sacred moment every builder, developer, architect, or founder will eventually experience.
It's the moment when everything catches fire — code, servers, wallet, soul — and you're left standing there like a dumbass holding a USB cable, wondering where it all went wrong.

This book was born in that moment.

Not after I succeeded.
Not after I scaled.
But after I faceplanted so hard, AWS sent me a sympathy coupon.

If you're looking for a neatly organized, sugar-coated roadmap to success,
you're in the wrong place.

There are thousands of LinkedIn influencers ready to sell you that lie for $29.99 a webinar.

This book is different.

It's the bruised, bloody, beer-stained field manual of someone who's fought real battles —
in the cloud, on the ground, sometimes flat on the floor.

I'm not here to show you how to avoid failure.
I'm here to teach you how to weaponize it.

Inside these pages, you'll find:

- ☑ Real disasters. (Yes, even the ones I still wake up sweating about.)
- ☑ Real technical lessons. (Actual tools and tactics — not motivational posters.)
- ☑ Real survival frameworks. (How to fail faster, recover smarter, and scale anyway.)

Plus enough sarcasm to keep you entertained
while your Lambda functions implode and your EC2 bills
threaten your blood pressure.

If you're a developer, cloud architect, solopreneur, or just a stubborn bastard trying to build something in this chaotic world —
this book is for you.

Welcome to the crash site.
Let's pick through the wreckage together —
and find out how real builders turn it into launchpads.

Let's fail like pros.
Let's f*cking go.

Part I — Code, Chaos, and Crying Inside

Chapter 1: When "It Works on My Machine" Became My Official Religion

---

Welcome to the Church of Localhost

There's a sacred moment every developer face -
when "It works on my machine" stops being an excuse and
becomes a full-blown religious doctrine.

Welcome to the Church of Localhost.
Population: everyone who's ever deployed something that
immediately caught fire.

The First Signs of Faith

It starts beautifully.

Fast. Clean. Elegant.
On your machine.

Then you deploy — and suddenly:

- 400 errors
- 502 Bad Gateway
- Servers screaming into the void

You mutter, refresh, pray.
"It works on my machine. Must be the environment's fault."

Thus, you are baptized.

The Real Problem Behind "It Works on My Machine"

When you trust local, you're blind to:

- Different environment variables
- Missing or misconfigured permissions
- Mocks lying through their fake teeth
- Hardcoded test data blessed by unknown gods
- Staging vs Production drift

Your machine is a fairy tale.
Production is a war zone.

My First Real Crash

I thought my Lambda + API Gateway setup was bulletproof.

Locally? Perfect.
AWS? **Deader than my weekend plans.**

The culprits?

- IAM policies missing scopes
- Lambda timeouts misconfigured
- Event payloads nothing like my test mocks

It was my first real dose of reality:
If it only works locally, it doesn't work.

⚔ 5 Brutal Lessons I Learned

1. **Local isn't real.**
   Always assume production is a separate beast.
2. **Environment variables must be explicit.**
   Inject them properly or expect fire.
3. **Mocks betray you.**
   Integration testing is survival, not luxury.
4. **CI/CD is your truth serum.**
   Automation will surface your sins early — or drown you later.
5. **Think two environments ahead.**
   If you don't, the next stage will eat you alive.

◉ Key Takeaways

- Local success means nothing without real-world testing.
- Automation saves you from yourself.
- Explicit configurations beat tribal memory.
- Assume every environment after yours is broken until proven otherwise.
- Shipping code is easy. Shipping systems is an art.

Chapter 2: I Accidentally Deleted Production. Here's What Happened Next.

The Day the Sky Fell

Every builder has a worst day.
Mine nuking production with a single script - during a live demo.

It wasn't sabotage. It wasn't even impressive.

It was a stupid cleanup task that went sideways, fast.

The Fatal Mistake

It started simple:

- Clear old environments.

- Save some AWS costs.

- Looks responsible.

One missed environment variable. One lazy wildcard. One click.

And just like that:

- Lambda functions? Gone.

- API Gateway configs? Wiped.

- DynamoDB tables? Vaporized.

- Logs? Nonexistent.

All because I trusted a script - and a little too much caffeine.

Immediate Fallout

Slack exploded with "WTF is happening?!"

Customers refreshing dashboards and got - nothing.

CTO's face? System error.

Meanwhile, I started at the AWS console – emptier than my soul.

The Real Loss: Trust

Infrastructure can be rebuilt.

Trust? Not so much.

Recovering services was painful. Recovering credibility was brutal.

🛠 How We (Barely) Recovered

- S3 backups saved most of the database snapshots.
- API Gateway configs manually rebuilt.
- Lambda functions restored from old deployment artifacts.
- Domain, certs, routes painfully re-verified.

14 hours, 3 Red Bulls, 2 panic attacks, 1 overpriced emergency pizza.

The Unforgivable Sins

- Scripts without dry-run safety.
- No true Infrastructure-as-Code.
- No environment isolation.
- Backups assumed, not tested.
- Zero chaos engineering drills.

---

5 Tactical Rules That Saved My Career

1. **Dry-Run Before You Destroy**
   - Never trust a script without a preview.
2. **Infrastructure-as-Code or Bust**
   - Consoles are cute—until 3 a.m. disasters.
3. **Hard Environment Isolation**
   - Separate accounts. Separate policies.
4. **Backup Restoration Must Be Tested**
   - A backup you can't restore is a fantasy.
5. **Assume You Are the Chaos Monkey**
   - Build systems that survive your own stupidity.

💼 My Personal "Oh Sh*t" Toolkit (After the Disaster)

- Automated backup verification scripts.
- Separate "break glass" IAM roles.
- Deployment snapshots archived externally.
- Mandatory peer review for destructive scripts.
- Printed disaster playbooks (internet dies too).

🧠 What They Don't Tell You About Failing Publicly

Destroying production isn't just technical.
It's **emotional warfare** inside your own mind:

- Shame.
- Doubt.
- Fear you'll never be trusted – or trust yourself- again.

The secret?

> **Speed, confidence, and resilience come back — if you survive long enough.**

Scars aren't liabilities. They're armor.

🔥 Key Takeaways

- Treat scripts like loaded weapons.
- Infrastructure must be rebuildable by anyone, anytime.

- Separate environments like you separate explosives.
- Test backup restorations, not just backups.
- Failure is your initiation—not your tombstone.

Chapter 3: The Serverless Mirage: Scaling, Failing, and Paying the Price

---

Welcome to the Desert of Serverless Dreams

When I first discovered serverless, I thought I'd found salvation.

No servers to patch.
No infrastructure to babysit.
Just beautiful, scalable functions dancing effortlessly on AWS.

I was drunk on the promise:
Easy. Cheap. Infinite.

It wasn't.

The Mirage They Sell You

The marketing pitch:

- Scale to millions without thinking.
- Only pay for what you use.
- Focus on code, not infrastructure.

Technically true — if you live inside a PowerPoint presentation.

In the real world, serverless quickly turns into:

- 🪲 Mysterious cost spikes
- 💧 Cold start hell
- 🌐 VPC networking nightmares
- 🫓 Observability black holes
- 🔋 Service limits smashing your face

My First Serverless Wake-Up Call

The project: a beautifully clean set of Lambda functions behind API Gateway.
The launch: traffic surged — and everything caught fire.

What hit us:

- Cold starts ballooned from 300ms to 8 seconds.
- API Gateway 429 throttling errors flooded users.
- VPC networking killed half the functions.
- Debugging distributed failures felt like reading tea leaves.
- AWS bill grew 5x overnight because we didn't tune memory settings.

Serverless scaled.
It scaled the pain, too.

The Hidden Enemies of Serverless

What they don't tell you:

- **Cold Starts Are Not Minor**
  At scale, they destroy UX.

- **APIs and Lambdas Hit Hard Limits**
  Throttling and concurrency will smash you early.
- **VPC Networking Is a Silent Killer**
  Lambdas inside VPCs timeout and die without perfect setup.
- **Observability Needs a New Art Form**
  CloudWatch alone is not enough. Distributed tracing is survival.
- **Misconfigured Memory = Financial Suicide**
  256MB isn't cheaper if your functions crawl.

⚔ 5 Brutal Serverless Truths I Learned the Hard Way

1. **Cold Starts Are a Scalability Tax**
   Pre-warm strategically or pay the latency bill.
2. **Throttling Will Happen — Budget for Retries**
   Architect for retries, not just success.
3. **VPC-Enabled Lambdas Need ENIs**
   And ENIs are slow to attach. Choose wisely.
4. **Observability Must Come First**
   X-Ray, structured logs, trace IDs — day one, not post-mortem.
5. **Cost Optimization Isn't Optional**
   Memory and duration tuning is survival, not tuning for "later."

🛠 How I Now Design Serverless Systems

- **Split Critical vs Non-Critical Functions**
  Async queues for non-critical, optimize critical paths brutally.

- **Pre-Warm Critical Endpoints**
  Scheduled warming to murder cold start latency.
- **Use Provisioned Concurrency Carefully**
  Only where cold starts are deadly.
- **Budget for Retries and Throttling**
  Always assume network calls fail once.
- **Cost Tune Memory vs Execution Time**
  Often cheaper to give functions more RAM and get them out faster.
- **Force Structured Logs and Tracing From Day One**
  No "we'll add it later" fairy tales.

Funny (Painful) Examples From the Field

- **Deployed a Lambda with VPC access** — 90% of requests timed out (ENI exhaustion, no alarms).
- **Shipped a payment API** — first 10 users loved it, next 100 throttled to death (default API Gateway burst limits).
- **Promised "serverless = cost savings"** — AWS bill quadrupled because of misconfigured memory and no queue batching.

Lessons burned into my soul.

🧠 Mindset Shift: Serverless Isn't "No Ops" — It's Different Ops

If you treat serverless like magic, it will magically destroy your project.

Serverless still demands:

- Capacity planning
- Cost modeling
- Monitoring setup
- Performance testing

It's not "free scaling."
It's "your bill, your outage, your problem."
Own it.

💧 Key Takeaways

- Serverless isn't simpler — it's differently complex.
- Cold starts, throttling, and VPC networking will punch you hard if you're naive.
- Monitoring, memory tuning, and retry logic are non-negotiable.
- Cost modeling is critical — or your bill will bleed you dry.
- Build like serverless will betray you — because sometimes, it will.

Chapter 4: CI/CD — Commit It / Cry Deeply

Where Dreams Go to Die

Building software is easy.
Shipping it safely?
That's where dreams go to die.

CI/CD — Continuous Integration and Continuous
Deployment — was sold as salvation:
push faster, catch problems earlier, automate the boring
parts.

And in theory, it's brilliant.
In reality?
It's how I discovered new depths of existential despair.

Why CI/CD Looked Like Heaven

At first, it felt like magic:

- Code commits triggered builds automatically.
- Tests ran without lifting a finger.
- Deployments zipped into the cloud before my coffee cooled.

No more tedious releases!
No more human error!

I was living the DevOps dream... for about three weeks.

How CI/CD Became My Personal Hell

Then the cracks appeared:

- A careless merge triggered a critical bug straight into production.
- Staging pipelines passed "green" because nobody updated the test suites.
- Secrets leaked into build logs because no one masked environment variables.
- Hotfixes collided with pending canary deployments — welcome to Frankenstein's prod.
- Deploys "succeeded" — while the app silently failed because health checks were garbage.

The biggest betrayal?
My blind trust in automation.

I turned pipelines into blindfolded snipers, firing code into production without thinking.

The Dumbest Mistakes I Personally Made

- Setting "auto-merge on green" for production branches.
- Skipping manual approvals because "it's just a tiny change."
- Not isolating deployment stages properly.
- Hardcoding environment variables into build configs.
- Believing "unit tests passed" meant the system would survive.

If stupidity had a trophy cabinet, I would've filled it that quarter.

⚔ 5 Brutal CI/CD Lessons Tattooed on My Soul

1. **Every Step Must Be Auditable**
   No logs = no trust. If it's not logged, it didn't happen.
2. **Production Requires a Human Checkpoint**
   Scripts miss what humans catch. Always double-check.
3. **Green Pipelines Mean Nothing Without Real Tests**
   Mock tests can pass while real systems bleed.
4. **Rollback Strategies Must Exist Before You Need Them**
   Canary, blue/green, alias shifting — whatever you pick, test it now.
5. **Secrets Management Isn't Optional**
   Vault, SSM, Secrets Manager — hardcoding is malpractice.

⚒ How I Now Build Pipelines (That Don't Try to Kill Me)

- **Separate Build, Test, and Deploy Phases Clearly**
  No sneaky magic from "build" to "prod."
- **Use Staging Like You Actually Care**
  Staging must mirror production — no shortcuts.
- **Implement Manual Approvals for Production**
  No PR, no deploy. Period.
- **Rollback on Failure Automatically**
  Roll forward sounds cool — until it nukes your database.

- **Encrypt All Environment Variables and Secrets**
  Secrets should never even *touch* a log file.
- **Alert Loudly on Pipeline Failures**
  Silent errors are deadlier than loud ones.

Funny (Painful) Moments I'll Never Forget

- A pipeline that "succeeded" — but deployed nothing. Nobody noticed for four days.
- Accidentally triggered 15 identical deployment jobs from a webhook misfire.
- Shipped a debug branch to production — homepage proudly showed "you shouldn't be seeing this!" to thousands of users.

Automation doesn't protect you.
It just delivers your mistakes at scale.

◉ Key Takeaways

- CI/CD is only as smart as the people who set it up.
- Trust, but verify — especially before production.
- Pipelines are weapons — treat them with respect, not laziness.
- Manual approvals aren't old-fashioned; they're survival.
- Logs, alerts, tests, and rollback plans aren't "extras" — they are non-negotiable.

Part II — The Art of Losing (and Still Moving Forward)

Chapter 5: Three-Day MVP? More Like Three-Month Bloody Marathon

---

The LinkedIn Fantasy

Everyone talks about building an MVP in a weekend.

Three days, they promise.
A couple all-nighters.
Hackathon vibes. Lots of pizza.

Then — product, users, funding!
Bullshit.

In reality?
Your "three-day MVP" turns into three months of duct-taping broken dreams together.
And that's if you're lucky.

Why the "Three-Day MVP" Myth Exists

The myth survives because it's beautiful to believe:

- Speed beats perfection.
- Customers love rough prototypes.
- Hustle harder, team optional.
- Launch now, fix later.

And to be fair — there's a sliver of truth.

But they don't tell you about:

- Technical debt deeper than the Mariana Trench.
- Stress fractures in every feature.
- Systems that collapse the second real users show up.

How My First "Weekend MVP" Became a Nightmare

Started simple:

- Build a backend.
- Expose a clean API.
- Mock the front end.
- Launch Monday.

Day 1:

- Core logic built.
- Backend API half-formed.
- Frontend still just wireframes.

Day 3:

- API barely validated input.
- Auth held together with duct tape and dreams.
- Zero error handling.
- Frontend throwing 401s like confetti.

But hey, it "worked" — until users touched it.

Then came the real marathon:

- Refactoring rushed API endpoints.
- Building real authentication flows.
- Designing actual database models.
- Writing tests to patch crater-sized holes.

- Untangling logic even I didn't understand anymore.

Three months later, we had something users could trust. **Barely.**

The Unseen Work Nobody Talks About

- Building admin dashboards
- Handling forgotten password flows
- Validating endless edge cases
- Managing infrastructure (DNS, SSL, hosting)
- Setting up monitoring and logging
- Tuning costs before AWS sends a "how are you still alive?" email

An MVP isn't "just a product."
It's the **entire experience** users expect — even when it's "minimal."
And minimum **doesn't mean broken.**

⚔ 5 Brutal MVP Lessons That Shattered My Optimism

1. **If Users Touch It, It Needs Error Handling**
   Users will break it in ways you can't imagine.
2. **Authentication Isn't Optional**
   "We'll add auth later" = "We'll get hacked immediately."
3. **The Backend Always Costs More Than You Plan**
   Models, migrations, validations, retries — none of it's free.

4. **Shipping Fast Doesn't Excuse Sloppy Architecture**
   Speed without discipline kills startups.
5. **MVP = Minimum Risk to Test an Idea, Not Minimum Effort**
   You're validating hypotheses, not building scrap piles.

🛠 How I Now Build MVPs (That Don't Become Nightmares)

- **Validate the Idea Manually First**
  Talk to users. Sketch workflows. No code until it's demanded.
- **Pick the Smallest, Most Valuable Workflow**
  Solve one painful problem extremely well.
- **Automate Infrastructure Early**
  Terraform, CDK, serverless — no castles on sand.
- **Treat MVP Code Like It'll Survive**
  Clean enough to live if it wins.
- **Instrument Everything**
  Metrics, logs, errors — because flying blind kills momentum.

Funny (Painful) Memories from My MVP Marathons

- User signup crashed if they entered emojis (thanks, UTF-8).
- Payment flow accepted duplicate payments (forgot idempotency).
- Forgot to enforce password resets — users shared accounts like Netflix subscriptions.

Each "oops" cost days.
Sometimes weeks.
Definitely sanity.

◉ Key Takeaways

- MVPs aren't weekend hacks — they're strategic experiments.
- Speed matters — but so do stability, security, and observability.
- Build MVPs like they'll succeed — or be ready to rebuild from scratch.
- Validate ideas fast, but build systems strong enough to survive user chaos.
- Your first version sets expectations — make it something you can live with.

Chapter 6: Debugging While Drunk — A Cautionary Tale

The "Brilliant" Idea

There are good ideas.
There are bad ideas.
And then there's:
"I can totally fix this production bug after three whiskeys."

This is the story of that third category —
the night I debugged a live system somewhere between
"functioning adult" and "sentient tequila sponge."

Spoiler:
I learned a lot.
Mostly about regret.

The Setup: A Perfect Storm of Ego and IPA

Weekend.
Small feature just went live.
I was at a bar, pretending to have work-life balance, when
Slack started lighting up.

Something broke. Bad.
Checkout flow down.
Support pinging.
Everyone freaking out.

I should've said:
"I'll fix it in the morning."

Instead, I said:
"Hold my drink."

Logging In While Logged Out of Common Sense

I opened my laptop at the bar:

- Public Wi-Fi? ☑
- No VPN? ☑
- Barely charged MacBook? ☑
- Slightly wobbly vision and way too much confidence? ☑

Perfect conditions for flawless disaster.

Within 15 minutes:

- SSH'd into the wrong server.
- Restarted a perfectly healthy service.
- Accidentally killed a queue worker.
- Deployed a hotfix — to the wrong branch.

At some point, I slurred "it's fine" loud enough that a stranger asked if I was okay.
I was not.

The Aftermath (a.k.a. Monday)

Sober.
Hungover.
Opening my laptop to view the crime scene:

- Checkout bug? Still alive.
- Half the logs? Missing — toggled off debug flags.
- Database? Several duplicate entries.
- Environment variable? Pushed to the repo. Unencrypted.

We spent most of Monday cleaning the mess.
I didn't speak much.
Just stared at my monitor like I was watching my own funeral on Zoom.

What I Should Have Done Instead

Reality check — alcohol and production systems **do not mix**.

What I should have done:

- Escalated to a sober teammate.
- Sent clear status updates and paused deploys.
- Disabled the feature toggle temporarily.
- Documented the issue and walked away.

What I actually did?
Waged war against a broken system…
while broken myself.

⚔ 5 Absolutely Unbreakable Rules I Learned That Night

1. **Never Touch Production While Intoxicated**
   Doesn't matter if it's one beer or five shots — your judgment is gone.
2. **Your Laptop Is Not a Lifeline at 1 AM**
   It's a liability unless you're sober and focused.
3. **Pride Is Not a PagerDuty Strategy**
   Let someone else take over. Your ego can wait.
4. **Have a Failsafe in Place Before Disaster Hits**
   Feature flags, circuit breakers, read-only modes — survival kits for your future stupid self.
5. **Apologize and Document Everything After the Fact**
   Owning your mistakes builds trust. Hiding them destroys it.

⚒ How I Now Handle Emergencies (Sober or Not)

- **Scheduled on-call rotations** with enforced escalation policies.
- **Access limits** at night and weekends unless explicitly authorized.
- **Feature toggles** ready to disable broken features without redeploying.
- **Slack automation** flags emotion-loaded words like "urgent," "shit," or "fucked."
- **Monitoring alerts** routed through centralized incident tooling with fallback contact plans.

Basically:
I assume Future Me will be tired, stupid, distracted, or drunk —
and I build systems that **don't require him to be a hero.**

The Funniest Sad Truth

This wasn't the only time I tried to be a hero.
But it was the last time I tried it with whiskey in my bloodstream.

Also:
My laptop still smells like regret and cheap scotch when it heats up.
A permanent reminder.

◍ Key Takeaways

- If you're under the influence, stay away from production — no exceptions.
- Just because you can access the system doesn't mean you should.
- Incidents need systems, not cowboy saviors.
- Pride kills more uptime than bugs ever will.
- Learn to say: **"I'm not in the right state to handle this — someone else should."**

Chapter 7: The $500 Bug That Cost $15,000 in Reputation

Not All Bugs Are Created Equal

Some bugs crash quietly in staging.
Some squeak into production and get patched fast.
And some?

Some bugs cost $500 to fix — and $15,000 in lost trust.

This is the story of how one "small" bug punched our business in the teeth —
and why I never underestimate tiny failures anymore.

The Bug That Looked Like "No Big Deal"

It started, like most mistakes, with a rushed feature tweak:

- Simple field validation.
- One line of JavaScript.
- A desperate sales team pushing for a live demo.

We "quick tested" it — translation: clicked around for ten minutes.
Pushed live.
It worked.

Mostly.

Except it didn't.

How It Broke Everything (Quietly)

The validation worked fine — if users filled out the form correctly the first time.

If they didn't?

- Session data quietly corrupted.
- Duplicate entries in the backend.
- Cart states misaligned.
- Payment attempts failed silently.
- Users got stuck, confused, or angry.

On the surface?
No obvious error.
In the logs?
A slow, creeping disaster.

When We Realized the Damage

First hour:

- Minor support tickets: "I can't checkout."

Third hour:

- Multiple abandoned carts.

End of day:

- A major client canceled a trial order.

By the end of the week:

- Lost revenue from abandoned carts.
- Lost months-long client deals.
- Word of our screw-up spreading like wildfire.

All from **one tiny bug**.
One "small" mistake.

⚔ 5 Lessons That Got Tattooed Into My Brain

1. **Small Bugs Compound Fast**
   Silent corruption is deadlier than loud crashes.
2. **Form Validation Is Not Cosmetic**
   It's critical infrastructure. Treat it like a battlefield.
3. **"It Works for Me" Means Nothing Without Real User Testing**
   Edge cases live in user chaos, not your unit tests.
4. **Fixing Code ≠ Fixing Damage**
   Trust lost is not easily bought back.
5. **Slow Failures Are Deadlier Than Hard Crashes**
   Bleeding quietly kills more than exploding loudly.

🛠 How I Build and Test Now (Because of That Bug)

- **Treat Frontend Validation Like Critical Infrastructure**
  No "just a UI thing" excuses.
- **Automate Full User Flows**
  Login, cart, checkout — simulate all journeys.
- **Chaos Test Forms**
  Invalid inputs, network dropouts, double-clicks — break it before users do.

- **Prioritize Recovery Flows**
  Design "what happens when users screw up" before polishing success paths.
- **Ship With Metrics on Key Actions**
  If cart conversions dip 5%, alarms scream.

Funny (Painful) Stats From That Incident

- Cart-to-checkout conversion dropped by **27%** before anyone noticed.
- Took **7 days** to stabilize orders and restore trust.
- Lost **3 months** of pipeline sales from reputation bleed.

All from **five lines** of sloppy JavaScript.
Five. Lines.

◉ Key Takeaways

- Small bugs can have enterprise-sized consequences.
- Validate every input, every flow — even the "obvious" ones.
- Recovery from failure must be designed, not improvised.
- Monitor critical user journeys continuously, not just uptime.
- Fixing the bug is easy. **Fixing the fallout is brutal.**

Chapter 8: Nobody Cares About Your Genius Startup Idea. Good.

The Brutal Truth

When you're deep in build mode, it's easy to believe your startup is **special**.
Different.
Revolutionary.

You imagine announcement tweets.
TechCrunch articles.
Investors begging for a piece.

Reality check:
Nobody cares.

And that's not bad news.
It's the best thing you could possibly hear — if you know how to use it.

Why "Nobody Cares" Is Actually Freedom

If no one cares yet, you're free:

- Free to experiment.
- Free to build without pressure.
- Free to discover what actually resonates — not what you think should.

The market isn't out to crush you.
It just doesn't know you exist.

Your job isn't to defend your idea.
It's to **make something so undeniable people can't ignore it anymore**.

My First Startup Delusion

I spent six months building a SaaS platform I was sure would "disrupt" the market:

- Clever tech.
- Beautiful UI.
- Slick branding.

When we launched:

- 34 visitors.
- 3 signups.
- 0 paying customers.

The idea wasn't bad.
It just wasn't painful enough to matter.

We built something nobody was asking for — and perfected a solution for an imaginary problem.

Why Execution Crushes Ideation Every Time

Ideas are cheap because:

- No commitment required.
- No punches from the real world.
- No facing users, objections, or real payments.

Execution?

- Forces you to talk to real humans.
- Forces you to solve real problems.
- Forces you to adapt — or die.

Success isn't about the idea.
It's about the evolution under pressure.

⚔ 5 Brutal Startup Truths I Learned the Hard Way

1. **No One Owes Your Idea Attention**
   Earn every second of mindshare.
2. **The Market Only Cares About Its Own Problems**
   Not your tech stack, not your hustle — just their pain, their wallets.
3. **The First Version Is Always Wrong**
   Assume it. Embrace it. Iterate fast.
4. **Feedback > Features**
   Talking to users beats shipping shiny buttons.
5. **Solve a Bleeding Problem, Not a Mild Inconvenience**
   People pay for aspirin, not vitamins.

🛠 How I Approach New Ideas Now

- **Interview Users Before Coding**
  20–30 raw conversations minimum.

- **Launch a Landing Page Before a Product**
  Measure real interest when you have nothing to offer.
- **Prototype the Simplest Possible Solution**
  If it takes six months to ship v1, it's too big.
- **Kill Ideas Ruthlessly If No One Bites**
  Move on. No shame.
- **Let Customer Pain Drive the Roadmap**
  Solve screams, not imaginary wants.

Funny (Painful) Memories From My Early "Genius" Projects

- Built a beautiful AI recommendation engine.
  Users just wanted a **simple filter button**.
- Developed complex gamification for a niche SaaS app.
  Users ignored it — they just needed a **faster CSV export**.
- Designed a slick multi-step signup flow.
  Conversion rate **dropped 50%**. A simple email box would've crushed it.

Every time, I thought users would be wowed.
Every time, they just wanted **the simplest damn thing that worked**.

💧 Key Takeaways

- Your startup idea is worthless until it solves a real, painful problem.
- Validation happens with users, not in your head.
- Nobody caring is an opportunity — not a rejection.

- Execution — fast, humble, painful — beats inspiration every time.
- Focus less on being clever, more on being **useful**.

Part III — Surviving Startup Life Without Selling Your Soul

Chapter 9: Money Is the Blood, Not the Soul

When Passion Meets Rent

People love talking about passion.
Vision.
Building cool things.

But when real bills hit your desk —
when vendors call, services charge, taxes bite —
you learn fast:

Passion doesn't pay invoices.
Money does.

Cash isn't the soul of your business.
Cash is the blood.
Without blood, you don't meditate your way back to life.
You die.

The Distillery Lesson: When Reality Punched First

I didn't learn about cashflow pain from SaaS dashboards.

I learned it standing in a real building:

- Real rent.
- Real vendors.
- Real taxes stacking up like little death threats.

Running the distillery wasn't about making a great product. It was about survival:

- Every fruit delivery had to be paid for — whether bottles sold or not.
- Every utility bill arrived — whether customers walked in or not.
- Every delay, tax rule, and equipment failure demanded cash — not passion.

No investor deck saved me.
No blog post about "founder mindset" fixed it.
Only cash flow mattered.
Only discipline mattered.

What Happens When Money Runs Tight

At first, it's not dramatic.

You shuffle bills.
Negotiate terms.
Dip into reserves.

Then the choices get uglier:

- Which supplier gets paid first?
- Which service gets cut off?
- Which customer refund will wreck your margin this month?

The pressure grinds you down.
It squeezes optimism until only realism survives.

The Real Cost of Cashflow Mistakes

When people say "lack of cashflow kills businesses," they make it sound like a numbers problem.

It's not.

It kills your:

- Time
- Focus
- Mental health

When money runs tight:

- You can't think creatively.
- You can't take risks.
- You can't plan long-term.
- You stop dreaming — and start surviving hour by hour.

Eventually?
You burn out.
Or worse — you stop caring.

⚔ 5 Lessons Cashflow Tattooed Into Me

1. **Cash Flow First, Everything Else After**
   No cash, no future. Period.
2. **Real Expenses Don't Care About Your Optimism**
   Bills are merciless. Optimism doesn't extend deadlines.

3. **Every Sale, Every Dollar Counts**
   Especially early. Especially when you're bleeding.
4. **Your Product Is Only as Good as Your Cash Resilience**
   Rough quarters will come. Can you survive them?
5. **Passion Without Discipline Is a Fast Track to Bankruptcy**
   Love the work — but respect the blood that keeps it alive.

🛠 How I Treat Money Now (Because I Had To)

- **Forecast Everything Monthly**
  Cash thresholds trigger alarms — emotionally and operationally.
- **Treat Every Dollar as Oxygen**
  More money = more time to fix, build, and survive.
- **Separate Enthusiasm From Liquidity**
  Loving your product doesn't pay server bills or taxes.
- **Build Systems That Survive Bad Months**
  Expect the worst. Build for survival first, dreams second.

Real (Painful) Memories

- Watching promising partnerships die because I couldn't afford to wait six months for "potential revenue."
- Doing the brutal math on how many bottles had to move just to survive a month — and realizing margins were thinner than I liked to admit.
- Paying salaries before paying myself — because **that's what leadership actually means**.

◉ Key Takeaways

- Cash isn't evil. Cash is freedom.
- Vision matters — but cashflow makes vision possible.
- No product survives reality without financial discipline.
- Passion without revenue is a hobby.
- Businesses don't die from lack of dreams. **They die from lack of cash.**

Chapter 10: The Day I Lost Everything I Built (And Why It Was the Best Thing)

Nobody Plans for the End

You start a project, a business, a dream — and you picture the success story:

- The launch.
- The traction.
- The proud milestones.

You don't imagine:

- The shutdown.
- The silence.
- The inventory you can't move.

But sometimes losing everything
is the only way you learn what really matters.

The End Came Slowly, Then All at Once

At first, it was alive:

- New product lines.
- Branding sessions.
- Late nights fine-tuning every last label font.

Then reality crept in:

- Sales fluctuated harder than forecasts.

- Regulations tightened.
- Margins shrank under logistics, licensing, and endless costs.
- Marketing returns evaporated campaign by campaign.

Month after month, the math refused to lie.
Hope carried it further than logic —
but eventually, even hope tapped out.

No optimism.
No effort.
Just slow bleed, then collapse.

What It Feels Like to Shut Down Something You Built

There's a silence no one talks about —
a specific, crushing silence when you realize:

"This isn't working. And it won't."

You turn off systems you spent months configuring.
Cancel licenses you fought to afford.
Tell suppliers, partners, friends:
It's over.

You pack away the dream.
Box by box.
Invoice by invoice.

It's like attending your own funeral —
except you have to sort the paperwork afterward.

The Worst Part Isn't Financial — It's Identity

For months, that business was my life:

- First thought in the morning.
- Last thought before sleep.
- The reason birthdays and weekends blurred away.

Shutting it down wasn't just losing money.
It was losing **identity**.

- Who was I if this failed?
- What did it say about me?
- What the hell was next?

Nobody teaches you how to bury a dream.
You learn by bleeding.

But Here's the Truth: That Failure Saved Me

Once you survive losing something you thought you couldn't live without?

You become dangerous.

You stop fearing:

- Small failures.
- Broken systems.
- Sunk costs.

You realize:

- Failure isn't death.
- Ego isn't survival.
- Flexibility is power.

When you have nothing left to protect,
you start building smart — not scared.

You chase real opportunities.
You build foundations for storms, not sunny days.

⚔ 5 Hard Lessons From Losing Everything

1. **Sunk Costs Are Sinking Ships**
   If the model's broken, fix it — or jump before you drown.
2. **Pride Will Starve You Faster Than Failure**
   Pretending it's not over will destroy you faster than admitting it.
3. **You Are Not Your Project**
   Skills, knowledge, grit — they survive even if this thing doesn't.
4. **Flexibility Beats Stubbornness Every Single Time**
   Markets shift. Customers vanish. Regulations crush. Adapt or die.
5. **Rock Bottom Is a Hell of a Foundation**
   Once you're fearless, you move smarter, faster, stronger.

🛠 How I Build Now (Because I Lost Before)

- **Test Markets Before Building Products**
  20–30 real conversations first.

- **Set Hard Stop Rules for New Ventures**
  Revenue, growth, profitability — clear thresholds or kill it.
- **Separate Identity From Projects**
  I'm not the business. I'm the builder.
- **Create Exit Strategies Early**
  Know when and how to walk away — tactically, not emotionally.
- **Expect Hard Seasons**
  Winter is always coming. I build with that in mind.

Funny (Painful) Aftermath

- Friends said "but it was going so well" — as I liquidated equipment at a loss.
- Found a box of old branded merch six months later. Donated it to Goodwill and laughed.
- Shutting down freed me up to build three better, faster, stronger businesses.

Killing a dream hurt.
Clinging to a dead one would have killed me faster.

🜂 Key Takeaways

- Failure is a phase, not a full stop.
- You are bigger than any single project.
- Pride kills. Adaptation saves.
- If it's dying, let it die — and learn.
- Real builders rise from ashes faster than they ever built castles.

Chapter 11: Scaling APIs Is Easy — Integrating Humans Is Not

Systems Follow Rules. People Don't.

Scaling backend systems is challenging — sure.
But at least it's predictable:

- Add compute.
- Tune performance.
- Watch logs.
- Fix and deploy.

Systems follow rules.

People?

- No rules.
- No logs.
- No retries.

I didn't manage people on paper.
But I had to manage the **impact of people** on everything I built.

And that's where it got messy.

Systems Scale. People Drift.

I've built APIs that handle thousands of requests per second.
I've watched them scale beautifully.

Then watched **one misaligned human** burn weeks of work —
not out of malice,
but out of confusion.

Or worse — **false confidence**.

I've had to:

- Rewrite features because someone misunderstood architecture.
- Patch last-minute logic based on half-guessed assumptions.
- Explain — for the fifteenth time — why rate limiting isn't a business decision.
- Watch arguments spiral because no one wanted to look dumb.

Nobody reported to me.
But they sure as hell impacted my systems.

The Hidden Cost of Human Misalignment

- Miscommunication adds more latency than any cold start ever could.
- Feature handoffs break without shared context.
- Feedback gets filtered through pride, insecurity, and Slack emojis.
- "Who's responsible for this?" becomes a detective game, not a README line.

I didn't need permission to lead.
I needed **clarity to survive**.

Because in a system with unclear ownership,
everything breaks silently —
until users feel it.

⚔ 5 Lessons I Learned Scaling With People, Not Over Them

1. **Documentation Isn't a Chore — It's Armor**
   Your README is your first line of defense.
2. **Assume No One Reads Slack the Same Way Twice**
   Written words are processed through caffeine levels and passive-aggressive energy.
3. **Responsibility Must Be Spoken, Not Implied**
   If you're working on it, say so. If you're not, say it louder.
4. **Hand-offs Need Logs, Not Just Vibes**
   Git history is not context. Document what changed, why, and what broke.
5. **Every Person Impacts the Architecture**
   Even — especially — the ones who don't touch code.

⚒ What I Do Differently Now

- **Over-Communicate in Writing**
  Ambiguity is expensive.
- **Leave Notes Like I'll Disappear Tomorrow**
  Because I might. Or they might.
- **Draw Diagrams, Even Bad Ones**
  Clarity over art. ASCII counts.

- **Expect Confusion — and Preempt It**
  Systems fail not because people are dumb,
  but because they **assumed** people wouldn't be.

Funny (Painful) Moments From the Human Layer

- Someone updated a config in staging, thinking it was production. Issue? A lowercase environment name.
- Spent two weeks undoing a "refactor" that renamed variables just to sound smarter.
- Had to explain — again — why "it worked locally" **doesn't count**. Screamed internally.

I wasn't a manager.
But I was the one who cleaned the mess.
Because **someone always has to**.

🔴 Key Takeaways

- You don't have to manage people to feel the pain they cause in systems.
- Clear ownership and brutal clarity save everyone — especially yourself.
- Every person adds entropy. Systems must absorb and guide it, not break under it.
- Communication isn't a soft skill — it's **infrastructure**.
- Build systems with humans in mind — because humans will always be part of them.

Chapter 12: Cloud Costs — The Silent Killer No One Warns You About

---

The Dream That Turned Into a Bill

When I first moved everything to the cloud, I thought I was being smart:

- Serverless functions? ☑
- Auto-scaling? ☑
- Pay only for what you use? ☑

It sounded like a dream.
Then I opened my AWS bill.

That dream?
Turned into a nightmare — in 15-minute billing increments.

Why Everyone Falls for the "Cheap Cloud" Lie

Cloud pricing looks harmless:

- $0.00001667 per invocation.
- $0.023 per GB-month of S3 storage.
- $3.50/month for a managed DNS zone.

Pocket change, right?

Until:

- You forget to clean up test resources.
- Your async queue retries itself into oblivion.
- You scale functions without tuning memory or timeout.
- You pump 10GB/day of debug logs into CloudWatch.
- A Lambda calls itself recursively for three days straight — and nobody notices.

Suddenly, you're not paying $12/month.
You're paying $312.

And you don't even know why.

My First "How The F*ck Is It That High" Bill

I once got slapped with a **$900 surprise** for what should've been a quiet serverless app.

Why?

- Someone turned on provisioned concurrency — and forgot.
- CloudWatch logs weren't capped.
- We ingested and stored every external webhook payload.
- A Lambda hot looped itself to death due to one stupid logic bug.

It ran beautifully.
It scaled instantly.
It burned money silently — like a polite little arsonist.

The Real Problem: Cloud Scales Usage — and Usage Scales Cost

The cloud scales beautifully.
But what it **really scales** is **usage**.
And what usage scales?

Bills.

There are no natural brakes unless you bolt them on yourself.
It's a casino with an open bar tab —
and AWS just thanks you for playing.

⚔ 5 Brutal Lessons Cloud Billing Taught Me

1. **Everything Has a Price — Even the "Free" Stuff**
   Free tiers end fast — and silently.
2. **Logs Are Not Free**
   CloudWatch is a bill disguised as a debug tool.
3. **Provisioned Services Cost You — Even If Idle**
   "Running but unused" still means "paying rent."
4. **Storage Is Cheap — Until It Isn't**
   Data hoarding backs up garbage at premium rates.
5. **Spiky Workloads Are Financial Landmines**
   Spikes trigger scaling, retries, and downstream charges before you blink.

🛠️ How I Build Now (Because of Those Bills)

- **Tag Every Resource**
  Cost owner + project — always.
- **Automate Weekly Cleanup Scripts**
  Zombie resources get nuked. No mercy.
- **Cap Logs and Monitor Ingestion Metrics**
  Financial errors are still errors.
- **Set Budget Alarms for Every Environment**
  Dev, staging, prod — tight leash everywhere.
- **Simulate Worst-Case Costs Before Production**
  Assume scaling succeeds — and kills your wallet — if unchecked.

Funny (Expensive) Memories

- Paid **$79** to store **200MB** of test logs for two months — forgot a retention setting.
- Enabled **X-Ray tracing across every Lambda** — turned the bill into a Christmas tree of regret.
- Let an S3 bucket host image uploads from a spam bot — **4TB later**, met "PUT request charges" the hard way.

💧 Key Takeaways

- The cloud doesn't punish bad architecture with errors — it punishes with bills.
- Logging, scaling, retries, and storage are silent money leaks.
- Cost optimization isn't "nice to have" — it's part of architecture.

- Budget alarms, aggressive cleanup, and cost modeling are mandatory.
- Great engineers know their **code** and their **cost footprint**.
Anything less is irresponsible.

Part IV — Winning Ugly

Chapter 13: Release Fast, Fail Faster, Recover Fastest

Speed Without Control Is Just Chaos

"Move fast and break things" sounds cool on a t-shirt.
Way less cool when your production system is bleeding out at 3 AM.

Shipping fast is powerful.
Necessary, even.

But if you don't design for **failure** — and **recovery** — you're not moving fast.
You're moving dumb.

The best builders don't just launch fast.
They **fail faster** and **recover fastest**.

Why "Just Ship It" Is Only Half the Story

Speed means nothing if you:

- Can't detect a bad release immediately.
- Can't roll it back in seconds.
- Can't contain the blast radius.
- Can't recover user trust after the outage.

Speed is a weapon.
Without control?
It's just **random fire in a crowded room**.

My First Fast Release Disaster

We had a minor UI tweak queued up.
Low risk. High reward.

Pushed it straight to production.

15 minutes later:

- Error rates spiked.
- Support exploded.
- Revenue flatlined.

All because one tiny frontend change
broke a tightly coupled backend validation flow.

Fast?
Yeah.
Fast and f*cked.

What Real "Move Fast" Should Mean

- Move fast through **small, safe, observable steps**.
- Design **failure paths** before launch.
- Know **exactly** how to undo what you ship.
- Make rollback part of deployment — **not emergency surgery**.

⚔ 5 Brutal Lessons About Release Velocity

1. **Releases Should Be Boring**
   If every launch feels like a cliff dive, you're doing it wrong.
2. **Rollback Plans Aren't Optional**
   Every deploy must have an abort button — automated, fast, tested.
3. **Blast Radius Must Be Contained**
   Feature flags, staged rollouts, canaries — precision tools for failure.
4. **Deployment ≠ Release**
   Shipping code doesn't mean exposing it. Separate them.
5. **Metrics and Alerts Must Be Wired to Every Launch**
   If you can't measure impact in minutes, you're blind.

🛠 How I Handle Releases Now (Because of The Pain)

- **Feature Flags Everywhere**
  Deploy code safely. Activate it only when ready.
- **Staged Rollouts**
  1% of users first. Then 10%. Full rollout only after confirmed survival.
- **Atomic Rollback Paths**
  Every branch cleanly revertible — fast, boring, drama-free.
- **Deploy Monitoring Built-In**
  Every deploy tied to fresh dashboards and alerts.
- **No Silent Launches**
  If it's live, it's announced. No exceptions. No surprises.

Funny (Painful) Fast-Release Memories

- Accidentally released a half-migrated database schema — 400 errors flooded in like biblical plagues.
- Pushed an API refactor on a Friday. Monitored it from a camping trip with no signal. **Never again.**
- Rolled out a "small" config change — redirected all prod traffic to a staging server. Oops.

Every one of these disasters could've been avoided **by respecting speed with recovery in mind**.

⬢ Key Takeaways

- Move fast — **but build your parachute first**.
- Releases should feel **uneventful** — that's maturity.
- Rollbacks should be **planned, tested, boring, and fast**.
- Monitoring isn't post-deploy — it's part of deployment.
- Failure is inevitable. **Recovery speed is what earns real respect.**

Chapter 14: Security Is Survival, Not a Trophy

Lock the Damn Door

Security was never a badge.
No audits. No fancy titles.

It was simple:

- If I screw up, everything burns.
- My apps.
- My users' trust.
- My money.
- My reputation.

I didn't treat security like a checklist.
I treated it like locking the front door at night —
because the world is real and full of thieves.

How I Learned to Care (Without the Buzzwords)

No dramatic hacker story.
No black hoodie cliches.

Just painful little lessons:

- Accidentally exposed credentials. Spent a night sweating and rotating them.
- Watched bots scrape an API I thought nobody cared about.
- Leaked internal IP addresses through sloppy error messages.

- Watched user trust evaporate faster than uptime after small mistakes.

It didn't take a disaster to scare me straight.
Just enough **close calls** to realize:
You don't get extra lives.

The Real Game of Security When You're Building Alone

- Nobody's coming to rescue you.
- Nobody cares if "you didn't mean" to leave a bucket public.
- Users won't forgive "small project" mistakes.

If you leak data? You're done.
If you get breached? You're done.
If you betray trust once? **You're done.**

No movie about it.
Just users moving on without you.

⚔ 5 Security Lessons Tattooed Onto My Brain

1. **Everything Public Gets Scanned Eventually**
   Test APIs, hidden routes — if it's online, it's hunted.
2. **Credentials Belong in Vaults, Not Repos**
   Not even private repos. Not even "temporary" commits.
3. **Don't Show Off Error Messages**
   Stack traces aren't cute — they're invitations.

4. **Minimal Permissions Everywhere**
   Read-only by default. Write access only when absolutely necessary.
   Admin should feel like carrying a loaded weapon.
5. **Logs Are Gold — Until They're a Liability**
   Log enough to debug.
   Not enough to leak PII when buckets get breached.

🛠 How I Build Now (Because of Those Close Calls)

- **Encrypt Everything That Moves**
  S3 uploads, database backups, even low-priority traffic.
- **Secrets Never Touch the Codebase**
  Parameter Stores, Secrets Manager, environment variables — always.
- **Assume Breach at Every Level**
  Plan for failure before building, not after.
- **Sanitize Logs Religiously**
  No leaking user IDs, tokens, emails — nothing.
- **Set Hard Permissions Even If It Annoys Me**
  Temporary annoyance beats permanent regret.

Funny (Painful) Moments in My Security Evolution

- Had an S3 bucket locked tight — but forgot the folder permissions inside.
  Bucket: secure. Files: wide open.
- Accidentally exposed a test admin endpoint hidden behind a "secret" URL.
  (Spoiler: security through obscurity is a f*cking joke.)

- Thought "small internal tools" didn't need HTTPS. Browser warnings scared testers away like I was hosting malware.

◉ Key Takeaways

- Security isn't for show. It's for survival.
- Treat systems like someone is always trying to break in — because they are.
- Stupidity, laziness, and assumptions kill faster than hackers.
- You don't need certifications to be secure.
- You just need **paranoia, discipline, and respect** for the internet's dark reality.

Chapter 15: The Myth of "Done"

The Moment That Never Comes

Early in my career, I believed there would be a moment —
a glorious, peaceful moment —
where I could lean back, sigh, and say:
"Finally. It's done."

Yeah.
That moment never came.

Because in building, in systems, in startups, in life —
nothing is ever truly done.

"Done" is a myth sold by project managers who need to file
status reports.
"Done" is a lie we tell ourselves so we can sleep at night.

Real builders know:

- Everything is temporary.
- Everything breaks.
- Everything needs iteration.

Always.

How I Learned It (Painfully)

First big project.
Months of work.

Launch day.
Champagne popping.

One week later:

- New feature requests flooding in.
- Bugs in edge cases we hadn't considered.
- Performance bottlenecks invisible at "demo" scale.

Two months later:

- Refactoring architecture for 10,000 users.

Six months later:

- Sunset discussions.
- Migration talks.
- Tech debt we hadn't admitted to yet.

I realized:
"Done" isn't a finish line.
It's just the starting gun for the next layer of problems.

Why the "Done" Mentality Is Dangerous

- It makes you lazy.
- It blinds you to weak spots.
- It makes you defensive about change.
- It turns necessary feedback into a threat.

Systems you call "done" today
become the liabilities you curse tomorrow.

What "Done" Really Means (When You Grow Up)

- Shipped **for now**.
- Working **at today's scale**.
- Stable enough **to shift attention elsewhere temporarily**.

It's never:

- Untouchable.
- Perfect.
- Finished forever.

If your system is alive — if users touch it —
it's either **evolving**
or **dying**.

There's no third option.

⚔ 5 Brutal Lessons I Learned About "Done"

1. **Every Release Is Just a Snapshot in Time**
   Celebrate it — but don't marry it.
2. **Tech Debt Starts the Moment You Deploy**
   Not years later. **Immediately.**
3. **What Works at 1X Will Strangle You at 10X**
   Scalability isn't a feature. It's a ticking debt.
4. **Users Change Faster Than Systems**
   Adapt or lose them. Fast.
5. **Architecture Is a Living Organism, Not a Monument**
   If you don't feed it, clean it, and evolve it — it rots.

🛠️ How I Build (Knowing "Done" Is a Lie)

- **Design Systems to Be Replaced, Not Worshipped**
  Build modules expecting them to get ripped out someday.
- **Expect Change Requests Before You Ship**
  Write systems ready to flex, not snap.
- **Celebrate Small "Done" Moments — Then Move Immediately**
  Party today. Iterate tomorrow.
- **Kill Dead Systems Fast**
  Dead weight costs more than ugly growth.
- **Document With Decay in Mind**
  Notes aren't to preserve perfection — they're maps for surviving wreckage.

Funny (Painful) Memories About "Done"

- Declared a dashboard "done" — users demanded mobile versions immediately.
- Launched a "final" API — two weeks later, had to version it for new response formats.
- Refactored the "last time" we'd touch a service — **three times** in the same year as scale exploded.

Every time I thought something was finished?
It was just ready for the next battle.

🜂 Key Takeaways

- "Done" is a checkpoint, not a destination.

- Systems survive through **adaptation**, not perfection.
- Tech debt starts the moment you stop thinking critically.
- Real builders love what they create — but are willing to **tear it down without hesitation**.
- Celebrate wins — but **keep your boots laced**.

Chapter 16: Burnout Isn't a Badge. It's a Warning Sign.

Stop Glorifying Self-Destruction

In tech — hell, in life — people love glamorizing burnout:

- "I worked 100 hours this week!"
- "I haven't slept properly in a month!"
- "I forgot what day it is!"

And somehow, that's supposed to sound impressive.
It's not impressive.
It's stupid.

Burnout isn't a badge of honor.
It's a **flashing red warning light** that you're about to wreck everything you've built — including yourself.

And when you crash?
Nobody's handing out medals.
They just step over the wreckage.

How I Learned (The Hard Way)

No single dramatic crash.
Just a slow, grinding bleed:

- Sleeping badly, working longer.
- Staring at screens without seeing them.
- Shipping half-broken features because "good enough for now."

- Snapping at people for asking basic questions.
- Watching the thrill of launches fade into numbness.

I kept pushing:

- One more week.
- One more project.
- One more client.

Until one day, I sat in front of my laptop for six hours —
and wrote exactly zero lines of meaningful code.

Not distracted.
Just empty.

Burnout doesn't arrive with sirens.
It sneaks in, steals your energy, creativity, resilience —
and leaves a hollow autopilot shell behind.

Why Burnout Is So Dangerous for Builders

- You still *look* productive — for a while.
- You still *meet* deadlines — by sacrificing quality.
- You still *say* "I'm fine" — even as everything inside rots.

By the time you realize how bad it is?
You're already deep into apathy, anger, exhaustion, and mistakes.

Burnout doesn't just slow you down.
It **poisons your work**.

⚔ 5 Brutal Lessons Burnout Taught Me

1. **The Brain Has a Battery**
   You can't run it on emergency mode forever.
2. **Quality Pays the First Price**
   Corners get cut. Tests get skipped. Bugs get born.
3. **Burnout Turns Passion Into Resentment**
   The things you loved become the things you hate.
4. **Rest Isn't Optional**
   It's maintenance — like oil changes for an engine.
5. **Nobody Cares How Much You Suffered**
   Only you live with the wreckage. Everyone else moves on.

🛠 How I Survive Work Now (Instead of Being Consumed by It)

- **Plan Rest Like Releases**
  Scheduled. Intentional. Non-negotiable.
- **Track Energy, Not Just Tasks**
  If I'm dragging three days straight, I intervene.
- **Separate Hard Work From Self-Destruction**
  Sprints are fine. Death marches are not.
- **Protect Focus Like It's Revenue**
  No pointless meetings. No death-by-notification.
- **Accept That Logging Off Is Sometimes the Most Productive Move**
  If the engine's overheating, you don't push harder — you fix it.

Funny (Sad) Burnout Moments

- Forgot my own birthday one year — too deep in code releases.
- Shipped a backend update that broke **100%** of all API calls — thanks, exhaustion.
- Took "vacation" — spent it lying on the couch, guilt-ridden and paralyzed.

Burnout doesn't make you stronger.
It makes you a **slower, stupider version of yourself**.

Nobody needs that.
Least of all you.

🌢 Key Takeaways

- Burnout isn't impressive. It's fatal if you let it fester.
- Hard work is noble. **Self-destruction is not.**
- Rest isn't weakness — it's **reloading your weapon**.
- Protect focus and energy as ruthlessly as uptime.
- If you don't fix burnout early, **it will fix you — permanently**.

Chapter 17: Fail Like a Pro

Master Failure — Or It Masters You

If there's one thing I learned from every crash, every bad release, every shutdown, every late-night rebuild — it's this:

Failure isn't optional.
Mastering it is.

The amateurs?

- Treat failure like shame.
- Hide it.
- Deny it.
- Let it rot them from the inside out.

The pros?

- Fail smarter.
- Fail faster.
- Fail louder.

And **keep moving**.

Because real builders don't die from failure.
They die from **silence**.

Why You Must Learn to Fail Properly

You're going to screw up.

Not once.
Not twice.
Relentlessly. Repeatedly.

You will:

- Merge bad code.
- Miss critical bugs.
- Misjudge costs.
- Misread users.
- Launch things nobody wants.
- Break things you thought were unbreakable.

That's normal.

What's deadly is pretending otherwise.
What's fatal is hiding from the free lessons failure offers —
if you're willing to bleed for them.

How I Learned to Fail Like a Professional

Every disaster taught me — but only when I faced it head-on:

- **Deleting production?**
  Taught me backup discipline.
- **Shipping broken APIs?**
  Taught me the difference between "tests pass" and "systems survive."
- **Running out of cash?**
  Taught me money isn't optional oxygen.
- **Burning out?**
  Taught me I'm no good to anyone dead inside.

I didn't learn these lessons from Medium posts.
I learned them bleeding in the field.

⚔️ 5 Rules for Failing Like a Pro

1. **Own the Failure Fast**
   No finger-pointing. No excuses.
   First words: "It's my fault. Let's fix it."
2. **Extract the Lesson Before Moving On**
   Don't just survive. Analyze. Post-mortem
   everything.
3. **Broadcast What You Learned**
   Share it loudly, transparently, fearlessly — with
   your team, your users, yourself.
4. **Build Resilience Systems, Not Fairy Tales**
   Assume failure. Build retries, rollbacks, escape
   hatches everywhere.
5. **Wear Scars Like Badges, Not Anchors**
   Scars mean you fought.
   Scars mean you adapted.
   Scars mean you're still standing.

What Failing Properly Looks Like

- Shipping a bug, fixing it fast, and telling users
  exactly what happened.
- Admitting when an architecture call was wrong —
  and refactoring without ego.
- Accepting that sometimes, despite best efforts, the
  market doesn't care — and pivoting without shame.
- Facing your worst mistakes not with regret — but
  with curiosity.

Every wrecked system is a classroom —
if you have the guts to sit in it.

Funny (Painful) Failures That Taught Me More Than Success Ever Did

- Spent three months building a feature nobody used — learned to validate faster.
- Burned $2,000 on a failed marketing campaign — learned not to trust "guaranteed traffic" pitches.
- Botched a database migration — learned the hard way why hourly snapshots matter.
- Overpromised, underdelivered — learned to respect my own limits **before** others punished me for it.

◉ Final Key Takeaways

- Failure is part of the builder's DNA. Pretending otherwise weakens you.
- Shame is dead weight. Lessons are fuel.
- Real success stacks failures so fast you outrun people still "planning perfectly."
- Loud scars beat quiet regrets every time.
- **If you're afraid to fail, you're already building slow enough to lose.**

Closing: Build Loud, Fail Proud

You Made It.

If you've read this far, you already know:

- There's no clean path.
- There's no safe map.
- There's no final "arrival."

You build.
You bleed.
You fix.
You fail.

And if you're smart?
You get faster at it.

You stop treating failures like shameful little secrets.
You stop looking for permission to move.
You stop apologizing for learning the hard way.

Because real builders?

- Fail more.
- Fail louder.
- Fail smarter.

And the ones who survive the longest?
They're not the ones who never crash.
They're the ones who crash harder, fix faster, and build
stronger from the wreckage every damn time.

If You Remember Nothing Else, Remember This:

- Launch when you're scared.
- Fix when you're tired.
- Adapt when you're proud.
- Rest when you're smart.
- Burn the past when it holds you back.
- Never confuse a single wreck with a full defeat.

Your failures aren't your shame.
They're your f*cking portfolio.

Go Build Something Worth Breaking

The world's full of cautious, quiet builders.
You won't remember their names.

Be the loud one.
Be the stubborn one.
Be the one who refused to stay down when shit went sideways.

- Build systems.
- Break expectations.
- Fail like a f*cking professional.

Because the only real failure?
Is staying silent.
Staying safe.
Staying invisible.

And that's not why you're here.

You're here to **build**.
Loud.
Proud.
Unstoppable.

Now get the hell out there —
and make the next disaster **worth surviving**.

If you bled and built with me here, the *AWS Cloud Mastery Series* will show you how to architect systems that survive even your worst days. Keep building. Keep breaking. Keep winning ugly.

Acknowledgments

This book wasn't written from a safe place.
It was built out of scars, long nights, dead systems, lost bets, and the stubborn refusal to stay down.

I didn't write it alone — even if it sometimes felt like it.

So, here's who I owe:

To every broken deployment, corrupted database, lost client, late-night debug session, and project that crashed harder than my caffeine tolerance —
thank you.
You taught me faster and harder than any success ever could.

To the builders who are too stubborn to quit, too honest to fake it, and too crazy to play it safe —
this is for you.
You are my people.
You are the real architects of everything worth creating.

To the few who believed in my madness when it made no sense —
and to the many who didn't —
you both gave me fuel.
You both made this necessary.

And finally, to the future me:
When you fail again — and you will —
I hope you open these pages, laugh bitterly, wipe the blood off your hands,
and remember:

You didn't come this far to build quietly.

About the Author

Souren Stepanyan is a builder, breaker, and stubborn survivor in the world of tech.
With years spent battling real-world systems, scaling impossible architectures, and bleeding through server crashes, he writes from the front lines — not from a sanitized, corporate distance.

When he's not fixing broken deployments at 2 A.M. or wrestling cloud bills into submission, you'll find him teaching others how to fail smarter, recover faster, and build systems that survive real chaos.

He believes scars are proof you tried, resilience matters more than credentials, and the only true failure is staying silent.

You can find him (and probably a few more battle stories) at:
www.sourenstepanyan.com

Also, by Souren Stepanyan

AWS Cloud Mastery Series: Building and Securing Applications

- **Mastering AWS Lambda: From Basics to Advanced Architectures**
- **Mastering Amazon S3: Comprehensive Guide to Cloud Storage and Data Management**
- **Mastering AWS IAM: Troubleshooting and Solutions**
- **Mastering AWS DynamoDB: Scalable NoSQL Solutions**
- **Mastering Amazon OpenSearch: Architecting High-Performance Search Systems on AWS**
- **Mastering Amazon Aurora: Architecting Scalable, Highly Available Cloud Databases**
- **Mastering AWS Neptune Analytics: Architecting In-Memory Graph Analytics Solutions with openCypher, Vector Search, and AWS Services**
- **Mastering Amazon API Gateway: Architecting Secure, Scalable APIs on AWS**
- **Mastering Amazon DocumentDB: Build, Scale, and Secure High-Performance NoSQL Applications on AWS**
- **Mastering Amazon MemoryDB: A Practical Guide for Developers and Architects**
- **AWS Databases for AI/ML: Architecting Intelligent Data Workflows**
- **Mastering AWS: Solving the Top Developer Challenges with S3, IAM, EC2, Lambda, and Cognito**

www.ingramcontent.com/pod-product-compliance
Lightning Source LLC
LaVergne TN
LVHW051715050326
832903LV00032B/4220